MEDITATION

East and West

HERMAN ADRIAN SPRUIT

EDITED BY ALAN R. KEMP

Hermitage Desktop Press
Vaughn, Washington

MEDITATION
East and West

HERMAN ADRIAN SPRUIT
EDITED BY ALAN R. KEMP

Hermitage Desktop Press
P.O. Box 167
Vaughn, WA 98394

ISBN: 978-0692509302
Library of Congress Control Number: 2015948934

Printed in the United States of America

TABLE OF CONTENTS

EDITORIAL NOTE v

FOREWORD.. ix

PREFACE... xi

DEDICATION xvi

Chapter 1–Getting through the Door 1

Chapter 2–Three Paths of Spiritual Unfoldment...... 6

Chapter 3–What of the Cost? 10

Chapter 4–The Gist of TM 13

Chapter 5–Mantramic Meditation 19

Chapter 6–The Power of Symbols 30

Chapter 7–Programmed for Living................................36

Chapter 8–Symbols from Far and Near......................42

Chapter 9–Spiritual Cleansing.......................................46

Chapter 10–Breaking Through to the Light 51

Chapter 11–Comparative Views of Meditation........56

Chapter 12–And What About Me?................................65

Chapter 13–The Ultimate Theological Deception..67

Chapter 14–Invisible Helpers...70

Chapter 15–Last Minute Tips 73

ABOUT ASCENSION 78

EDITORIAL NOTE

Herman Adrian Spruit was an uncommon visionary who appeared on the scene when the field of ministry in the U.S. was firmly rooted in religious conservatism (Spruit, 1979; 2015). Himself a prominent Methodist minister (indeed, he was a representative at the founding of the World Council of Churches), he would leave the comfort of his denominational home to embark on a quest (Keizer, 1976).

By 1951, he had become unfulfilled by mainstream Christianity and resigned from ministry in the Methodist church. Feeling drawn to mysticism, he became associated with Ernest Holmes, and briefly served as Executive Secretary of Holmes' Church of Religious Science (Melton, 1991).

It was during his time with the Science of Mind Church that Spruit also chanced on an alternative form of Catholic Christianity and the opportunity to blend the Dutch Old Catholic heritage of his father with direct mystical experience (Melton, 1991). No longer tied to mainstream Christianity, he felt free to explore alternative forms of spirituality.

He came upon the work of Charles Leadbeater and other teachers linked to the esoterically oriented Theosophical Society (Melton, 1991). Leadbeater was an influential member of the Theosophical Society, who was also an early Presiding Bishop of the Liberal Catholic Church–a Church which traces its lineage, or "apostolic succession," through the Dutch Old Catholic Church, which separated from Rome in the early 1730s.

In the early 1950s, Spruit met Charles Hampton at the Liberal Catholic Pro-Cathedral in Hollywood, California. At the time, Hampton was the Regionary Bishop for the Liberal Catholic Church in the United States and Canada. Hampton apparently saw promise in Spruit, for he would ordain him as a deacon in 1955, a priest in 1956, and ultimately consecrated him a bishop in 1957 (Melton, 1991).

In 1965, Bishop Spruit became the head of Robert Raleigh's independent Christian Catholic Church (Melton, 1991). In 1968, he changed the name of that body to the Catholic Apostolic Church of Antioch–Malabar Rite, to affirm its Antiochean, Syrian Orthodox lineage, which had come to the U.S. from India through Archbishop Joseph René Vilatte. Of a liberal bent, Spruit's "Church of Antioch" was among the first churches to ordain women to the priesthood and to establish an esoterically-oriented seminary.

After Archbishop Herman's passing, the organization he founded continued under the leadership of his life partner, Archbishop Meri Louise Reynolds Spruit, then under the guidance of Archbishop Richard Gundrey, and now under the leadership of an entirely new generation.

A new organization, the Ascension Alliance, emerged after this new generation assumed leadership of Archbishop Herman's former organization. And, it is the Alliance's contention that it has inherited Archbishop Herman's "charism"–that is, his spiritual mission, ministry, and mantle, or religious authority.

In 2015, the Alliance acquired an original copy of Archbishop Herman's little volume on meditation, *Meditation: Transcendental and Otherwise*. Transcendental Meditation, or TM, had been taught to thousands of people by Maharishi Mahesh Yogi during a series of world tours from 1958-1965. By the time Archbishop Herman published his book, the TM movement had become a social phenomenon in the U.S. and was clearly on his mind (Spruit, 1970).

Maharishi Mahesh Yogi during a 1979 visit to the Maharishi University of Management in Fairfield, Iowa. Released into the public domain by the photographer, Keithbob.

Transcendental Meditation, as originally brought to the West, is not nearly as popular today as it was when Archbishop Herman wrote his *Meditation* book. So, in an effort to address the widest possible audience we changed the subtitle of the present edition from *Transcendental and Otherwise* to *East and West*. This reflects the evolving social reality and also honors Herman's admonition to seek Truth wherever it may be found.

References

Keizer, L. S. (1976). *The wandering bishops: Heralds of a new Christianity.* Santa Cruz, CA: Academy of Arts and Humanities.

Melton, J. G. (1991). *The encyclopedia of American religions: A comprehensive study of the major religious groups in the United States and Canada.* Tarrytown, NY: Triumph Books.

Spruit, H. A. (1970). *Meditation: Transcendental and Otherwise.* Cambria, CA: Church of Antioch Press.

Spruit, H. A. (1979; 2015). *The Sacramentarion.* 1979 Edition, Mountain View, CA: published privately by the author. 2015 edition, Vaughn, WA: Hermitage Desktop Press.

FOREWORD

Have you ever asked the questions "Why meditate? What's in it for me?" If you have, this book may be for you. *Meditation: East and West* is a recently uncovered little jewel written by Archbishop Herman Adrian Spruit. It is a concise, but comprehensive, little work that reflects his deep conviction that meditation and prayer are essential to the experience of inner communion with the Divine.

Herman visited Houston, Texas in early 1980 to address the group of seminarians I was a part of. We were on fire with the love of God and were anxious to serve. At the Church of Divine Presence, under the leadership of Bishop John Rankin, we were about to embark on a course of study that would eventually take us to ordination in the Catholic apostolic priesthood–for men and women, single and married–at a time when such "innovation" was almost unheard of. Such was his vision.

When Archbishop Herman made that visit we got a "crash course" on his wisdom and his vast fund of knowledge. On subsequent visits he kept that fire ignited. He taught us the basic methodology of meditation and we would practice it in depth while he was with us. He taught us to lose ourselves during the mystery and magic of our experiences and what followed was a state of consciousness that few of us could ever have anticipated. These experiences became the focal point of many conversations.

Herman had a "way" with words. As you yourself read the text, let the melody flow over you as a gentle breeze, refreshing and renewing your Spirit. It will.

This book is a treasure. Let it to take you where it will. Enjoy!!!

Archbishop Patsy Grubbs
Presiding Bishop, Ascension Alliance
August 20, 2015

PREFACE

It may come as a surprise to most people that according to a recent National Institutes of Health survey, almost 20 million American adults are engaged in meditation of some sort. Herman Adrian Spruit understood the need of his day, and in 1970, when Transcendental Meditation was sweeping the country, he saw a need to contextualize how and where meditation can fit into the lives of people.

It is clear to me, in reading this book, that Herman, as I prefer to call him, had a regular practice of meditation that led him into the silence in which there is only awareness of awareness itself. No thought, no feelings, only unbounded awareness. This is a place in our inner landscape that is free of worry, thoughts or ideas. It is a place of all possibilities—unbounded because it is not attached to anything. It is a place that St. Theresa of Avila knew well when she called it her "interior castle" and it was a place well known to St. Paul, who called it the "peace that passes all understanding." It was a place known to the psalmist of psalm 46:10 when he says, "be still and know that I am God."

Herman understood the need for this generation, and future generations, to understand that transcending ordinary experience is not just a privilege for monks, nuns or other religious, it is our birthright as children of God. In his day, millions of people learned Transcendental Meditation, and their experiences were profound and life changing. He began to think not of a specific technique or method as the ultimate, but instead sought to look for the experience of transcendence in many traditions and techniques as being legitimate pathways to silence.

It was theologian Paul Tillich who developed a theology that saw God not as a being, but as the "ground of all being." In this manner, being-ness itself is not a quality, but a state of life. As the ground of all being, the Divine could be present in all things. In the silence St. Theresa of Avila tells us, the Presence of God awaits us. In that Presence, we are lifted into the life of God at a fundamental level of life. In her book, "Spiritual Relations," St. Teresa describes the following experience:

> My soul at once becomes recollected and I enter the state of quiet or that of rapture, so that I can use none of my faculties and senses ... everything is stilled, and the soul is left in a state of great quiet and deep satisfaction.

This is the experience of the transcendent that is available to all of us.

Herman wanted to make that simple point clear, and he further wanted to encourage people to find ways to experience that peace—through meditative techniques as well as deep prayer. He shows us that this tradition can be found in the East as well as the West, and that it remains a crown jewel in the Christian tradition, even if not well known.

A lot has changed since this book was first written. Over 20 million people practice meditation, yoga, and breath work. Thousands of school children in school districts across the U.S. now practice meditation as part of their school day. In some countries, like Equador, even the Army teaches meditation to the troops as a way to reduce stress. As of this writing, over 200,000 of Equador's military personnel are learning Transcendental Meditation. People of all levels of society practice yoga and breathing to calm the mind and body. In today's health conscious society, health of mind and soul are beginning to find a central place in medicine and in a healthy lifestyle.

In Columbia, Father Gabriel Mejia has rescued tens of thousands of abandoned children from the streets and a life of drugs and violence, and through education and meditation he has helped them create new lives for themselves. The power of meditation to positively change direction is nothing short of a miracle. Father Mejia says:

> *The basic therapy is love. Love is the imperial medicine for any illness or disorder ... When a child closes his eyes and begins to meditate they open themselves to the field of all possibilities ... The world opens for the child. And then the child discovers their essential nature, which is love.*

Indeed, love is not an emotion—it is who we are. In the experience of transcendence—which is available to all of us—we are faced with the unbounded awareness that we are indeed love, that God is love, and that our lives are transformed through love. We were created by God in love, are sustained by God in love, and will return to Love when our lives are over.

To experience the love of God through transcendence is something that Our Lady of Medjugorje wanted for pilgrims. She told them that it is better to pray the rosary slowly, with feeling, than to move through it quickly. As one may quickly experience, this slow practice of the rosary leads to transcendence.

Herman's life was a life dedicated to raising people above the ordinary, above "churchianity," and into a life of devotion and purity. His wisdom frequently found a home in the many people who were part of the Church of Antioch, and now the Ascension Alliance and Community of Ascensionists. While this book may have been originally released in 1970, its republication comes at an important time, when many are seeking to rediscover the Christian tradition of transcendence, silence, and contemplation.

Many are seeking to become "monks in the world" and the practice of meditation helps to infuse the silence of the transcendent into everyday life and activity. Many seek to experience it for the quietness and refreshing rest it provides to mind and body. Still others experience it as a way to come closer to the Presence of God in their lives. I encourage you, the reader, to find a way to experience this silence for yourself, that you may enrich your life, and the lives of others, with the inspiration, clarity, and positive benefits that such a practice can bring to all aspects of your life. I leave you with the words of a prayer contained at the beginning of a 14th century book of instruction to monks on the mystical path—"The Cloud of Unknowing,"

O God, all hearts are open to you
You perceive my desire
Nothing is hidden from you
Purify the thoughts of my heart
with the gift of your Spirit, that I may love you
with a perfect love and give you the praise
you deserve. Amen.

Bishop Michael Adams
Ordinariate of Spiritus Christi
Ascension Alliance
August 22, 2015

DEDICATION

Archbishop Herman published this book in 1970, when he was still with his first wife, Helene Seymour, and living in Cambria, CA. Indeed, in 1976 he would consecrate her as a bishop in the Catholic "apostolic succession," among the first women so consecrated in modern history. On the title page of the original edition of this little book he wrote the following dedication:

This little volume is dedicated to my wife, Helen, in appreciative recognition of her loving and persistent encouragement for me to commit some of my thoughts to paper.

Herman Adrian Spruit, Ph.D., Sc.D.

Chapter 1–Getting through the Door

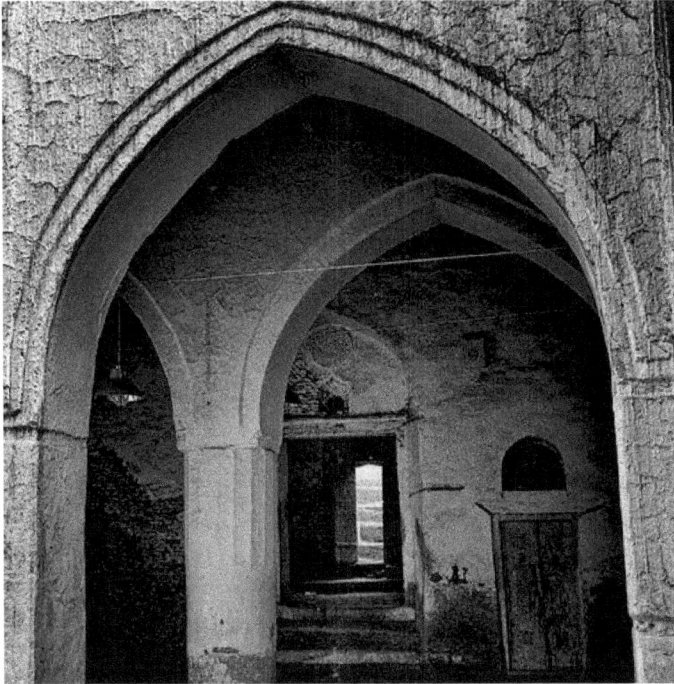

Back door in Yemen. Copyright © 2014 Rod Waddington. Used by permission of the photographer under Creative Commons Attribution.

Meditation seems to be the thing. It is both a term and practice we meet everywhere in the whole of the worlds of philosophy and religion. Even those far removed from profession or interest in either philosophy or religion look to it as a last way out. The standard Christian, hobbled by his limited vision and unable to ascend beyond the levels of New Testament mysticism, still finds some charm in the idea of meditation. We find that same

1

interest among the more sophisticated and informed Christians. Whether your conversation is with Yogis, or Sufis, Vedanta, Bahai, "metaphysicians," or a baker's dozen of other configurations of religious practice, meditation is always an accepted and acceptable modality and a secret "open sesame" of spiritual aspiration.

The virtues of meditation are extolled in books and pamphlets without number by a never-ending procession of writers and speakers, whose wisdom drops from their mouths and drips from their pens.

Why then, in the face of all this, would we want to add another tome? There are two reasons.

First, there are some who would find it easier to listen to me rather than to another. So, I write to them.

Second, this little book is projected as a popular summary for people who are eager to get started and find a way to make meditation work for them. Having tried much by way of religion in the hope for peace of mind and a clear inner light, meditation may, indeed, be their last try prior to kissing religion "goodbye" once and for all. Yes, this book is intended for the practical person, not the philosophical theorist, who wants and needs to bring him or herself into the bright orbit of the Divine Presence.

Beyond the scope of this little volume, there lie many other fields to conquer. The whole area of meditation might be compared to a continent of vast proportions. Like the surface of the moon, it has been really touched by only a few truly knowing souls.

Once you have exhausted the range of this book and find yourself reaching out to more scholarly tomes that will be a day of joy for me. I will know that I have served my purpose in encouraging you to go on further into something so really worthy of your best.

"What is the great Aeonian goal?"

"The joy of going on ..."

Well, then, what is meditation?

Any decent dictionary will tell you at least as much as this: Meditation is both discourse and contemplation.

Yes, discourse, indeed. "Meditation" is a word that has suffered much and been misused often. Years ago they called them sermonettes— these brief, vapid, somnolescent drippings of anemic pulpit oratory. Now, they call them "Meditations." Most of these homiletic offerings bear no resemblance to that which we would call "Meditation." Whenever, in a church advertisement, I spy this word "meditation" as intended pulpit fare, like the priest and the Levite, I pass by on the other side. Used in that sense, let us retire the term "meditation" as a synonym for discourse.

Contemplation comes close to the meaning of meditation. In fact, "contemplation" is the child whose father was concentration and the mother, meditation.

Meditation in its full and popular acceptance includes a fair sized bushel of a number of approaches, systems, and disciplines–as you will see and learn.

In its most inferior meaning, we see it, as we behold an incomplete and complacent person, who "meditates," comfortably seated in a soft chair, blowing smoke rings from his cigarette, while his mind drifts aimlessly and passively from one subject to another.

At the other extreme we find a mature aspirant, who uses meditation to direct actively his awareness on a chosen them, without deviation or a forgetting of it, hold it before his minds eye for a required length of time. By the way, here you have a good beginning definition of meditation. It is more than that. But is at least this much.

Having met the two opposing poles of what meditation represents, we might say that most of the rest of us would place somewhere between. We see in meditation a technique by which we can enter into contact with divinity and succeed in our attempt to solicit divinity's leadership in solving the most burning problems of our lives.

It has been well said that one great aim of meditation is to develop an ability of entering into a process of creative thought, where object and subject become joined into one. An attempt to enlarge this definition by placing it under the microscope of our imagination might yield some interesting ideas. It would mean that, if better health were the object of your search, meditation would be the process in which your idea of health and the enjoyment of it would become one. Suppose you are in search of a God like capacity for wisdom and love. In meditation you would find the ability so to focus on the love and wisdom of God that, in time, you would become a living and walking expression of the wisdom and love of God.

Before we hammer away some more on the definitions and purposes of meditation, I will switch, for a bit, to one account of what meditation has done for me.

The subtle directive influence of meditation has taken me past that fuzzy world of twilight, where most of us live most of the time, through that crack in the universe between daylight and dark into a world not merely other than our own, but of an entirely different order of reality–and without mescaline, LSD, or cannabis. It is a world of different gods, more adequate and respectable. It is a world of different post mortem fates. It is a state of being in which the very metaphysical presuppositions differ. Space does more than conform to Euclidean geometry. Time goes beyond forming a continuous unidirectional flow. Causation does not conform to Aristotelian logic. Humankind is not differentiated from the non-human or life from death. All the alternatives are subjected to the synthesis of the Hegelian dictum. Here I found the materials and skills to build more stately mansions for my soul.

Chapter 2–Three Paths of Spiritual Unfoldment

"Thames Path North of Sandford Lock." Copyright © 2011 , Derek Harver. Used and adapted by permission of the photographer under Creative Commons Attribution.

What a tremendously vast and overwhelming demand there is in our time for that which people call "spiritual unfoldment!" That quest may be part of your search, too.

The goal of "spiritual unfoldment" is, of course, not too well defined. It may involve the cultivation of ESP, parapsychology, spiritualism, necromancy, and the ability to toy with the shady side of magic. And then, if nay also be a genuine hunger and eager pursuit for true spiritual stature.

To all these and sundries we have a solemn word or counsel. On the face of it, your search is not as involved as it may seem, on the surface, that is. In all, there are no more than three techniques or modalities you need to follow. Whether you seek the blessed state of Samadhi, cosmic consciousness, or any and all of the lesser skills, rewards, or attainments within the realm of the mysteries, three ways you must follow and no more. Follow them without let up or interference, and you will move close, very close, to the shaper of your destiny.

The first of these techniques is meditation–you guessed correctly. Stay with it until you seem to have plumbed its greatest depths and gone to the full extent of its farthest boundaries.

When you have explored the full meaning of meditation and have put into practice all you have learned, then go on to the second technique, which is meditation.

Finally, when you have fully exhausted these previous exposures could offer, then you are ready for the third step. You must enter even more deeply into meditation.

If, at that time, the goals you sought to attain through meditation have not been attained, you must follow a further word of counsel. Continue to meditate either until the objective has been reached or a worthier one has been revealed to you.

One no less than Pascal once said, "All the evils of life have fallen on us, because men will not sit down quietly in a room." And that, friend, is the beginning of meditation–to sit down quietly in a room.

Once, a long while ago, someone asked me to give the strongest argument I knew for meditation. I could answer no more than this, "There is no argument for meditation. Try it, and see for yourself what may happen."

Our home, "Horizons Unlimited" stands on a promontory no more than a cable-tows length from the mighty Pacific, with piney woods of the Cambrian hills losing themselves in the deep surf below. The sundeck encircling our house for the full extent of the seaward view provides a setting with never ending fascination for fruitful meditation. With the moonlit waves of the azure blue Pacific washing the picturesque shores of Pelican Cove, God is closer than reach and grasp. Sitting there on frequent nightly exposures, wrapped in the Presence of the Lover of my soul, I enter into a world of exultation, where sleep, even, has lost its claim and meaning. And it was meditation that offered the key and opened the door to the inner side of beauty and bliss. Charisma, indeed! I want no other!

After a side trip into poetry born out of reality, I come to give you the real point of my story. The central heart of infinite calm can just as well be reached on occasions not so filled with wonder and awe. In the jail cell, perhaps, or on a bed of pain, even in the confusion and harassments of contemporary existence that kind of breakthrough is always the greatest and finest potential, of your whole life and world.

However rich, meditation does not reveal the full secret of its deepest mysteries. These must be felt. Just what is it? There are moments when the mind cannot discern whether it is the human crashing into the sacred precincts of the Divine, or whether it is God seeking dominion in the territory of humankind, so long kept locked to His sway and care. Meditation is the fulcrum on which is set the lever of the celestial potential, which slumbers in the heart of humankind. It is the miracle of union of which the elders have spoken, but which humankind must find for itself in each generation.

In meditation lies the power to change both lives and circumstances. No game is ever lost, so long as you have one more move. Meditation may be your last and winning move.

I heard it long ago. And now I have forgotten who spoke the words. Authorship, however, does not matter, so long as you recall the message, "The silence is where we come to grips with reality." The silence comes to us all, either imposed from without or selected by our own volition. The one voluntarily chosen is the one that yields the rich rewards.

Chapter 3–What of the Cost?

"Railway station Trollhättan in Västra Götaland County, Sweden." Copyright ©
2012 Nils Oberg. Used by permission of the photographer under Creative
Commons Attribution.

The train with the free rides just left the station. From
this point on, as I understand the fine print, there are
no free rides.

And what of the cost of meditation?

Let's answer this one by going the long way
around. Let's make some inquiry to pick up a few
basic ideas about meditation. What is it? How may it
be used? And, what is the manner by which you may
use it to your profit?

Flipping through the pages of a book written not
only by a man who is one of my favorite authors, but

also is one of the leading philosophers of our time, Manly Palmer Hall, I find one definition which breaks down, naturally and normally into four parts. (1) Meditation is an inward contemplation of divine realities. (2) The subjects of meditation are the aspects of truth. (3) Truth may be perceived and known only when the student is in a tranquil state. (4) There must be no tension or effort. Here we have method, philosophy, description, and instruction, all in our succinct sentences. Here we see that meditation is an art and a science, requiring as much solid preparation and solid dedication and study as every other important branch of human progress.

Looking over the shoulders of those who have had some ideas and opinions on meditation, we find this: "Meditation is the ability to rule your mind under all circumstances. It is the dynamic retention of your awareness on a chosen theme or subject. It is the ability to maintain unswervingly your awareness on a chosen theme for as long as you desire to continue with the same."

This gives a fifth dimension to those offered by Manly P. Hall. It is the idea of discipline spelled with a capital letter "D."

In our study we have now come to the place where we may embalm and forever lay to rest the old saw that "anyone can meditate."

Neither you nor I find it possible to swim the English Channel. To do so would require many long years of practice and discipline, plus a rugged constitution. And to walk on the moon calls for more than the mere purchase of a space travel ticket. Even as there are laws governing the physical manifestations of physical life, so are there laws governing the invisible manifestations of life. *The process of thinking and feeling into a subject, which is the heart and life of meditation,* is subject to laws far beyond the full extent of the concrete mind.

What are the conditions you should follow to have a reasonable promise of getting through to the Light as a result of studying and entering into meditation? Treat these thoughts, ideas, suggestions, and disciplines with the same sincerity and application as you did with the bread and butter courses at school.

If you want to argue points, bless you, I will have no time for you. Simply buy another copy and give it to an associate of yours who, like you, is mired in argumentation. Then, let's have the two of you have at it.

Some give their souls to the divine, some their life, some offer their work, some their money. A few consecrate all of themselves, and they have—soul, life, work, wealth—these are the true children of God. Others give nothing. These, whatever their position, power, and riches are for the divine purpose valueless cyphers.

This book was inspired and written for those who aspire to utter consecrate and full submission and consecration to the divine.

The cost?

Chapter 4–The Gist of TM

Maharishi Mahesh Yogi, the founder of TM. Copyright © 1973 Harald Bischoff. Used by permission of the photographer under Creative Commons Attribution.

The demand for books, classes, and records expounding the virtues and ways of Transcendental Meditation have been fanned into a million dollar business and claiming the attention of ever growing armies of spiritually hungry people.

Even though in its authorized and orthodox version it is not my thing, I want it to have its day in court. And being an eclectic with touches of the pragmatist, I want us to examine it for the virtues it holds for us.

The results claimed for it border on the astounding, even to the point of claiming it as ta technique for the addict in his quest for victory over drug problems. And clinical evidence is available to convince the scoffer.

Looking at TM dispassionately and with a scientific bent of mind, it is apparent to me that God has chosen it to help some of these His children during perilous days. Since some of the principles espoused by TM are applicable to the larger field of meditation, why not detour through this territory?

The final and ultimate aim of TM is to make it possible for the student to discover the reality of the Kingdom of Heaven as a fact that lies within one's self.

And with this we jump into the analogies, explanation, and justification offered by the promulgators of TM.

Looking at a tree we soon become aware of the outer and inner aspects of its life. The outer part consists of the trunk, branches, and leaves. The inner part is that which lies beneath the surface. The life force and nutrients, which reside in the soil are absorbed by the sap and transmitted to all parts of the tree.

Should a tree suffer from ills, which attack it, any damage sustained is speedily repaired by the tree itself, so long as the roots are healthy and the soil continues to give forth its richness.

Like the tree, humankind derives life and nourishment, which sustains its being, from a field or ground, which is not part of the body, but which is transmitted through the inner parts of its being–even as the ground transmits energy to the roots of the tree.

That mysterious field which provides for, feeds, and sustains human life, we shall call the transcendental field or the ground of our existence. This transcendent field is the basis of all life, subtle and gross, inner and outer, absolute and relative. Looking at human life, the gross body is the objective field of existence. The inner nature of humankind is the subjective field of existence. The source of the life and strength of humankind is the transcendent or absolute field of existence.

The goal of all religion, the aim of all seekers, the instinctive cry of everyone is knowledge of, communication with, and union with the transcendent or absolute field of existence–the ground of being.

The purpose of TM is to help seekers establish direct communication with this transcendent field. The purpose of this form of meditation is to penetrate to the deeper aspects of one's own inner life, help one find his or her own absolute field. It should be possible to touch the wellspring of one's own being, to absorb its richness, and to have it infused into the whole of one's life.

Unfortunately, humankind has lost the ability to gaze inwardly and observe his or her own true self. Having lost the capacity for insight into his or her inner and more vital nature, the range of experience is limited to the level of the surface, the gross, and the relative. It is as though humankind has allowed itself to become imprisoned.

Humankind's liberation from this imprisonment depends on the ability to break the hold of the senses on the mind freedom to move into other directions. This, as might be assumed, is dreadfully difficult to achieve.

Across the ages methods have evolved to allow oneself to be removed from the tantalizing grip of the world of objects and circumstances, which claim the attention through the sense. Among Christian s, prayer, good works, and devotion are relied upon as essential techniques. Eastern masters suggest seclusion, discipline, and concentration. The main purpose of these techniques is to learn control over the elusive sense and emotional forces and impel them to move in the right direction.

The main difficulty with these standard approaches is that mind being a wandering monkey or, to chance the picture, like a bit of mercury on a polished surface, escapes the limits of even the most rigorous discipline. Systems of conscious discipline are like a rocket that is chained to its pad, binding it fast, while keeping it pointed in the desired direction. Tying the rocket down only opposes and defeats the power locked within it, which are desired to push the rocket free from these strictures.

Disciplines and methods of concentration are effective at times and have their limited value. But their effectiveness is not universally and predictably true. That being the case, what other help is there?

TM holds that the mind, left to its own devices, will always prefer, be attracted to, and gravitate in the direction of the greatest measure of happiness. It is not necessary to force it to hold its attention in the direction of attractive goals. The mind is inclined to focus on them automatically. The only thing needed to take advantage of this natural inclination is a vehicle

16

of some sort, which will take it quickly to the Source it seeks.

To act as such a vehicle TM uses the medium of sound. It teaches that the vibrations crated by certain sounds and the mental images it creates make contact with the Source. Eventually this vibration, having united with the Source, reaches the absolute or transcendent field. In the course of its journey, the vibrations, which may have been released by lesser desires become more and more refined and, thus, more potent.

In TM the attention is directed inward and carried to the field, and is most naturally inclined to find that which it seeks. At last it arrives at the final threshold, transcending it, it crosses the boundary line between the subtlest field of relative and conditioned existence and moves into the eternal and absolute ocean of pure being.

This state is humankind's natural state, that perfect joy, the Kingdom of Heaven of which Jesus spoke. And having reached it, it is propelled back to transform humankind's conditioned state of being.

All our troubles and difficulties arise because of our lack of contact with that inner realm of True Life. By our return to communication with the ultimate state of being, the process of living reverses itself. A new process comes into being, gradually resolving the misery of our days and the terrors of our nights. This is the direct way to the divine presence according to TM.

The old routines of sacrifice and a life of overcoming do have their own reward. But they are not the short4est pat to inner peace and outward, creative usefulness.

As you have assumed by this time, in TM it is not required to practice austere disciplines or to develop superior powers of concentration. Nor is it advised that one be devoted to a set of routines or habits that may be strange to one's way of life or environmental conditions. The mind is set free from conscious control, is cast loose from the moorings of set patterns, and is free to hone in on its own targets.

The vehicle upon which the mind is borne into the transcendent realm must be carefully selected. It must be a special sound. It must be produced by the aspirant him or herself.

The training program of TM involves itself in teaching the student the proper intonation of that sound. This technique and its employment is part of a course offered by the teachers of TM. We, of course, do not intend to step into their territory or teach their courses. For the purposes of this book, this is not required. Our main concern in this presentation is to present to you this very popular program of meditation. In subsequent chapters we will point out its use in other applications.

Chapter 5–Mantramic Meditation

Om Mani Padme Hum in Tibetan script (2007). Released into the public domain by the artist, Nux.

The suggestion of using sound waves released by the human voice for constructive purposes is not a new discovery for the compendium of occult and mystical resources. In general, it was this approach that is said to have caused the walls of Jericho to come tumbling down. Lobsang Romp, in his readable books has called repeated attention to this phenomenon. A scholar of the labor of Lama A. Govinda gives much space to the idea of the sounding of the AUM as a mantramic meditative device. Christian sacramentalists who have gone beyond the shallow interpretation know well what power resources come into play in the singing of the KYRIE. The theurigical literature abounds with instructions on the purposeful and creative use of sound generated by the human voice. Many injunctions are given "to speak the word" and to "speak the word with power." Gurus spend long hours in training their chelas in the many applications and uses of this aspect of the sacred science. Brown Landone, that contemporary mystic, gave much instruction on finding the proper voice pitch for the most effective use of sound invocations. In the literature of Yoga we find entire sections dealing with this under the heading of "Mantra Yoga."

A mantra is a verbal symbol or spiritual formula. Usually its efficacy is increased if it is expressed in a language not known to the meditator. As far as languages go, their value in the use of mantras may be considered as follows, in a descending order of importance: Sanskrit, Greek, Hebrew, English, and Latin.

If in conjunction with verbal symbols visual image is used, it may be said that a higher degree of psychic energy is released or utilized and directed toward the fulfillment of the ideal that is sought. The regular, sustained, and disciplined practice of such audio-visual concentration has the effect of directing thought energy along definite and productive spiritual pathways. It produces a lift in the consciousness of the meditator, directs the individual toward union with the divine, and seeks to reach out toward the fulfillment of desirable and productive objectives.

A good mantra for the beginner is this, "AUM SHANTI, SHANTI, SHANTI." Translated from the Sanskrit, this would mean, "God is ineffable, Peace, Peace, Peace."

Suggestions for its use are as follows: find a comfortable and relaxed condition, not so relaxing as to put you in a drowsy mood, and practice a few deep breaths. Now relax your voice in the lower

20

range of your normal conversational, speaking, voice, as you would speak conversationally with a good friend. In that tone of voice repeat the mantra in Sanskrit form several times. Repeat this mantra but raise the pitch of your voice a tone higher. Do this for a total of five succeeding tones, each on slightly higher than the previous one. The purpose of this is to give yourself an opportunity to find the tone, which, to you, appears to be the most productive. Depend on the inner Presence to help you select the correct tone. Caution: Do not let sounds originate at the throat level. In the manner of good public speakers, use your diaphragm as a sounding board.

Properly, a guru should observe your practice. His trained ear and consciousness would be able quickly to select your proper tone. But since you may be doing this in the privacy of your own surroundings, you must depend on the Guru of Gurus to lead you in the selection of your right tone. With the prayerful recognition of this Presence and continued practice for a little while, you will succeed in finding that tone of peace, harmony, and spiritual action.

In the use of mantra meditation, for that matter any kind of meditation, always aim for the highest level and the most meaningful results. Get into the habit of living on high spiritual planes. A good aim for which to try is the desire of breathing through into the Light, find a personal assurance of the gift of healing as an operating force within you, pursue the continued growth of soul and spirit power within you, etc.

If you have decided on the goal, which is to occupy your attention for a time, try making a mental picture of it. Keep that picture in mind as you sound your Shanti mantra.

I recall using this one time when faced by severe financial limitation. Knowing that is a sin and insult to God to be poor, that God wanted me to have enough, and a little to spare, that God was my loving companion, I pictured myself praying with deep gratitude for the abundance that was mine. There was that deep "gut feeling" that I had several thousand dollars in the bank. Each time I worked with the mantra I sustained that feeling of praise for God's generosity with me. I did this kind of spiritual work for about ten minutes both morning and night. To recap, first, I recreated the picture in my mind, centering on God as the Giver; next, I assumed a relaxed position; then, I inhaled deeply a few times; fourth, I did my Shanti mantra for about ten minutes; in closing, I paused for a minute, breathing in and exhaling deeply for a few times. With this I returned to my usual vocation. As I did, I knew that my wok had gone forth in the transcendental field, the ground of my existence. I kept his up, without fail, for nine days. Near the end of the nine-day period I received a very generous check in a rather large set of figures. Like and earthquake, shock waves in lesser amounts kept coming in for several days in the form of additional checks.

Why nine days? There seems to be some magic in that number. It is the harvest number. Roman Catholics are known for their novenas–nine days of prayer for a particular purpose. It is of vital importance that you continue these rhythmic mantras for an unbroken period. If you forget to do your work one day, break off, wait two or three days, and then start over again. Never extend one mantra meditation for a period of more than twenty-one days.

The most used, least understood, most maligned, and most abused form of mantramic meditation, used by millions of Roman Catholics every day is the rosary.

In some quarters there remains a considerable backwash of prejudice about the rosary, all because some people have abused its values. That is about as intelligent a foundation for the rejection of a certain practice as it would be to stop eating because some people have degenerated into gluttony.

For a long time I was among those who had strong reservations, not only to the use of the rosary, but to any emphasis on the Blessed Mother as an object of devotion. In God's good time I learned that any form of religious prejudice is a sign of spiritual immaturity and a bar to effective spiritual development. Now, there is much gratitude and joy in my heart for the blessings and inspirations provided to me and those around me by means of the rosary.

I will resist the temptation to philosophize on the theological assumptions that deal with the Blessed Mother. (Editor's note: *A free Catholic concise liturgy: And other useful writings*, is a book authored by the editor of this volume and published by Hermitage Desktop Press, which provides detailed information about the traditional ways to pray the rosary). We digress far enough, however, to shed just a small ray of light on this subject. Until recently, Protestantism has been guilty of keeping hidden this very dynamic aspect of universal religion. It has been forgotten that on this plane of manifestation God operates on a bi-polar basis, as both male and female.

The Father is the Creative, male, aspect of divinity. The Blessed Mother, as many religions do, should be looked upon as the productive and manifesting aspect of deity. It is through the medium of the Blessed Mother that demonstration is attained. That which we seek in prayer and meditation is brought into being by the Father God and, then, is brought into our experience and possession by the Mother God.

Most of our prayers are directed to the Father and, therefore fail their ultimate purpose and direction. Which brings to mind an observation made by Jesus on the cause of our ineffectiveness in prayer, "Ye receive not, because you ask amiss." Yes, in spite of our unscientific methods of prayer, we do get some results. The grace and love of God is sufficient to find ways. However, in praying as we do, we resort to inefficient methods. And from what I observe as a scientist in the whole economy of nature, is that God always selects the most efficient means for the fulfillment of his/her purposes.

The rosary is one long step in the direction of correcting one of our basic errors of spiritual living and thinking. Using it may very well help to put our own little spiritual world back into harmony and balance.

24

There are two distinct occasions that stand out in my life, when recourse to the rosary more than saved the day. The waves of life around and about me had become so turbulent that I had become exceedingly fearful of the security of my little ship of life. Not only my life, but that of members of my immediate family was in danger. Only after all of my remedies had been exhausted, I turned to the rosary. Sparing you from exposure to too much information, I will say that this mantramic meditational modality saw me though shoals and dangers and gave me smooth sailing in calm and sunny waters.

History records many verifiable accounts of vast wonders produced through the concerted use of the rosary. At one time it served to banish the black plague from Europe. The Battle of Lepanto in 1571, in which Christian forces triumphed over the Turks, is historically credited to the use of this devotional technique.

For the help of the beginner, there is a simple set of instructions, in which we turn to the so-called "joyful mysteries."

First day–Spend a little time sorting out your confused aims, drives, hopes, and ambitions and determine what, if anything, you really want from life, the one objective which is above everything else. You might imagine that you had a lucky wishing ring, one that would be capable of fulfilling your one greatest desire. If you owned such a ring, what would you ask for? Let *that* one desire be the objective to zero in on as the object of this rosary type of meditation.

Sitting quietly and in a relaxed manner, breathing deeply and rhythmically "plug in" your set of imagination. Perhaps with eyes closed, visualize the Angel of the Lord coming to visit you, even as he did with Mary. See him speaking to you, see his lips moving, see the word forming, try to hear them, knowing that he is promising you the fulfillment of your wish. Accept this as a fact, do not waver or doubt. At the proper time this wish *WILL* become reality for you.

Keep this picture in mind as you commence with an abbreviated form of the rosary. First, say the "Gloria Patri" (Glory be to the Father, and to the Son, and to the Holy Spirit, Amen). If somewhere you have learned a tune for this chant, use it.

Next, you will repeat the Ave Maria five times, using this positive, "new age," reformulation, "Hail Mary, full of grace, the Lord is with you; blessed are you among women, and blessed is the fruit of thy whom, Jesus. Holy Mary, Mother of God, teach us now to lead our lives in love."

Conclude with the Lord's Prayer ("Our Father, which art in heaven, hallowed by thy name. Thy will be done on earth as it is in heaven. Give us this day our daily bread. Forgive us our trespasses as we forgive those who trespass against us. Lead us not into temptation, but deliver us from evil, for thine is the kingdom, the power, and the glory forever, amen"). You may sing it if you wish.

The entire cycle should be repeated five times. All the while, you must keep your angel picture in mind. If your attention is distracted, the cycle must be commenced again. When finished, pause for a moment of quiet, a few deep breaths, and go about your duties. Be assured that your manta will go forth into the transcendental field.

Second Day–Think of people who are very close to you, in incarnation or out of it, who would be the ones most entitled to hearing of some great news that has come into your life. "Plugging in" your imagination yet again, see yourself visiting these people or calling them by phone to tell them of the great and wonderful news the Angel of the Lord brought to you on the previous day.

Next, holding on to this picture, repeat the full cycle of the rosary in the same way you did on the previous day.

Mary's visitation with her cousin Elizabeth is the scriptural background for this picture.

It is quite obvious that this technique of devotion will do much to teach you something of the art of concentration. And, it will increase your mental stability, if nothing else. To hold in mind a firm picture and, at the same time, recite a mantra is good discipline. But it will achieve far more than this.

Third day–You are now moving closer into the circle of fulfillment. Life is beginning to test you to see if you are worthy of the boon you desire. At this point, visualize, "see," imagine as reality that which you seek and are working for. Mentally and emotionally enjoy this as a fact as much as Mary exulted in her newborn child.

"Though like a wanderer, the Sun gone down. Darkness be over me, my rest a stone; Yet, in my dreams, I'd see ..."

When this image reaches its highest degree of concreteness, start with your cycle of five rosary mantras. If your attention is broken, begin all over again.

Fourth day–This is the day of relaxed meditation. Having "received" your gift on the day before, it is now yours to do with as you wish. Now give it back to God, for Him-Her to bless, to hold, to return, to use as He-She desires.

This surrender of the gift is a vital phase of this cycle of meditation. You may think of this as a psychological game. Perhaps it is. But it is a gave that seeks to follow the devious ways and convolutions of the tricky human mind. The experience of many, who have tried this in practical life/laboratory situations shows that it works.

In the full impact of this mood of surrender, now enter into the five rosary sections.

Biblical correspondence here is the "Presentation of Jesus" in the Temple.

Fifth day–It will seem, time and again, that not only the picture of fulfillment but that even the hope of realization is lost, that something which appeared so very real on that third day. The effort at renewal of the picture must be made time and time again. Never give up the blessed assurance of realization. It may come as a thief in the night. It may come by unexpected routes. It may even be found among the animalistic tendencies of stable existence. Don't limit the channels.

The Bible reference is, "Jesus lost and found."

When you have recovered your vision, enter upon your cycle of rosary prayers.

After a few days of surcease, commence your cycle again with the same project until the aim is made real or you are shown a better way.

In addition to this discipline, there are two further ones using the rosary, known as the "Sorrowful," "Glorious," and "Luminous," mysteries.

Chapter 6–The Power of Symbols

Creation of the Sun and Moon by Michelangelo (c. 1512) surrounded by the symbols of various religions. Copyright © 2013 Blok Glo. Used by permission of the compiler under Creative Commons Attribution.

TM has opened some new and long closed doors in this great field of meditation. It has added new dimensions and taught us new lessons.

Most systems take for granted a bipolar scheme, in which the meditative process is involved. One of these is the God/human polarity. Simplified, it is made up of the following construct. A person meditates, disciplining his or her thinking, concentrating on deity, hoping in this way to reach the divine reality, expecting, thereby, to incur the response of divinity.

There is another such polarity, the conscious/subconscious mind polarity. In this scheme, it is assumed that the subconscious mind is a vast reservoir of almost unlimited potential, ready, under the proper conditions, to unload its wealth into the life of the lucky meditator. Like so many pseudo-religious modalities, it is a half truth and, therefor, not a dependable approach.

TM comes into our experience as a corrective. It convinces us of the validity of a three-pronged approach. In TM the aim of meditation is to reach the transcendental field, the ground of existence. From this comes and it transmits its powers to the vital aspects of life by way of the inner self of humankind.

In both the shanti mantras and in the rosary this insight is put to effective use. The outer mind, the conscious self, shapes the desired picture. In the sounding of the mantra the picture is transmitted to the Source of all Light and Truth, which, in time, returns the fulfilled desire. In the case of the rosary, the picture is beamed to the Blessed Mother of the Universe. The meditation completed, an immaculate conception having taken place, the fulfillment comes back to the conscious person by way of his or her inner self.

This ground of existence is neither conscious nor unconscious. It is above and beyond any known kind of consciousness. Perhaps the term "hyperconsciousness" could describe it. It is akin to what Max Freedom Long called the "High Self."

There is one resource or agency available to us, which is known to reach the hyperconscious realm almost without fail. This particular modality is known as "The Symbol."

The most highly sophisticated and stylized form of meditation employing the use of symbols is the basic form of Christian worship, i.e. the celebration of the "Divine Liturgy" (Orthodox terminology), "Holy Eucharist," or "Mass" (to use Anglican and Roman Catholic terminology). The average Christian may be surprised to hear their normal worship pattern so described. It is our conviction that the Divine Liturgy or Mass is capable of achieving more than any other meditational modality known to us. In my estimation, it is the most metaphysical and transcendental discipline of which we have any knowledge. Since a separate volume in this series is intended, we will detour around the subject. We will, however, bring to you some of the lesser modalities in this context. Their use will bring much strength and growth to you.

Meanwhile, we should put in mind one of the most vital axioms in the whole of a textbook on spiritual practice, "Consciousness may decidedly affect physical matter."

And the next is even more significant, i.e., "Meditation draws you automatically into the matter transforming area of the spiritual."

These thoughts draw us automatically into the single most important aspect of meditation. Although you may not attain through meditation what, at first, you desired, the fact that you are drawn into the area of the divine consciousness outweighs all other considerations. The physical circumstances can and do subject themselves to modification. And, the modification is in keeping with the demands of your highest good. Exposure and release into areas of higher awareness and understanding will open for you new vistas, possibilities, and solutions. In the event of unfulfilled desires, never give way to discouragement. Look for and find the new light, the better leads, and the greater opportunities that present themselves.

Perhaps, the best and most fruitful type of meditation would be the one that is not attached to any specific good or desire. There being something within you that knows and understands, turn yourself loose in the knowledge that the transcendental field will furnish that which your True Being demands.

To this end, we find a happy source, rich in meditative harvest in the use of symbolism. These symbols are the instrument so capable of slipping through those cracks between daylight and dark, between wakefulness and sleep. These will hold the door open long enough to allow the light of new understanding to filter back into your world of everyday affairs and transforming it with a new glow.

Much valid information has come from many sources pointing to the validity and effectiveness of symbols in meditation. Among these are the Huna Research Associates and the Biometric Foundation. They have assisted many to a fuller life in the recommendation of a certain type of symbol consisting of a circle with a dot in the center, a cross, and a triangle.

All of us are too well aware of the wide gap that exists between our potential and the actual levels of performance. Each of us has a potential output far greater than our production. What a boon it would be for us to bring our lives somewhere near to the top level of our capacities! Concerned about this, the groups just mentioned, have produced a meditative program, which is intended to bridge the gap. Let us briefly take a look at the program.

Set aside a period of meditation of fifteen minutes for both mornings and evenings. Being comfortably seated, or relaxing in bed, for a period of five minutes, keep your mind centered on the symbol of a ring with a dot in the center. For five additional minutes hold your mind on an equal-armed cross. During a final five minutes hold your mind focused on an equilateral triangle. Do this each morning and night for three weeks. If one day is missed, drop the entire program, wait a few days, and begin again.

In this period of time, a subliminal connection, or channel, will have been set up between the actual and the potential. Through this connection psychic energy waves will exert a "tug of war" effect on your low grade "actual" with the effect that it is being elevated to higher performance levels. Best of all, it will free your productive capacities from the tyranny of the many emotional booby traps we know so well.

In the Christian tradition, it is well to activate this program twice each year–during each of the penitential seasons of Advent and Lent.

This routine is considerably enhanced by adding the transcendental dimension.

For about five minutes, both morning and night, commence with the Shanti Mantra and conclude the period with the Lord's Prayer.

Some have found it helpful to draw these symbols on white cardboard, to look at them during meditation.

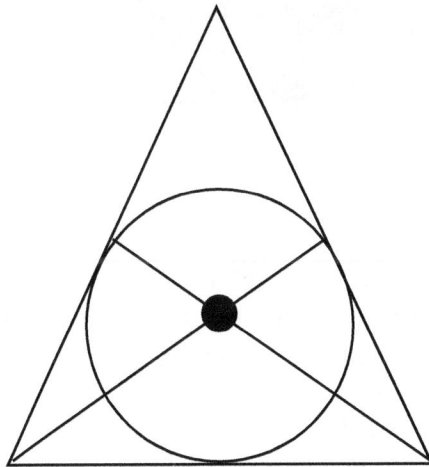

Chapter 7–Programmed for Living

"Simple Living, Interior of Replica of Thoreau's Cabin." Copyright © 2006 Tom Stohlberg. Used and adapted by permission of the photographer under Creative Commons Attribution.

Ages ago, as we began our long journey through many incarnations, at that far off point, which, for many of us was the beginning of time, each of us were programmed for an exciting course of action. It was intended as the scenic route to ultimate fulfillment. Our kit included all the devices and instruments to land us at the point of our ultimate goal in the swiftest possible way. Lest something go afoul, we were cut in the a program directing us into units of understanding plain enough to follow by the dullest in the crowd. Stalled as we are, on a trip that was to have been completed many lives ago, we can only conjecture as to the cause of the delay. From where we stand, it seems that someone started tinkering with the computer, with the result that the message got garbled with static.

In time, our knowledge of the program was lost, including the means of translating any residue of meaningful information to our understanding. Hoping for some kind of signal, humankind has been floundering on the high seas of confusion, biding our time and waiting for better days.

Fortunately for all humankind, someone not only managed to fix the computer but got the program back on keel. Yes, we are referring to Carl Jung, the noted Swiss psychiatrist, whose research for over fifty years resulted in the ability to regain direction. By a process so painful and tedious only a true scientist could endure, his work has been telling us about the essential program under which we operate. Yes, he speaks about the unconscious and archetypes, and other wonderful concepts.

What his learned presentations amount to is that within us there are sources of insight, which, if contacted and used, have the capacity to get us going again. Within our inner depths, we have archetypal sources of wisdom, which might help us find our bearings. And, one of the ways of reaching these archetypes is with the help of symbols.

The findings of this Jungian school have assured us, and our own experience has confirmed, is that the structure of the Christian Sacraments, particularly the Mass, is tops among the tools with which anyone can reach the archetypal deposits within the self. And so, the interrupted journey to the stars can resume once again.

Casual participation in sacramental occasions will be nominally helpful. But using these in the spirit of TM vastly enhances their value to the individual.

For a ride into the world of meditation that takes you into the high stakes country, try some parts of this sacramental route. Pick yourself a "right" kind of church for this trip. It could be Independent Catholic, Old Catholic, Episcopal, Orthodox, or even Roman Catholic. Remember, you are not trying this for philosophical reasons, but to use one of their services as a springboard for meditative action.

Follow the service. Be on the lookout for some part of it that interest you, excites you, rings a bell with you. Make part of it the subject of your meditation. Let that meditation lead you slowly, almost unnoticed, into your deep inner world of archetypal reality. It may be no more than the incense that is curling upward. Ask yourself some questions about its meaning and purpose. Give the inner self time to answer. Perhaps the incense bothers and annoys you. What could be the meaning of this? It might be a directive to stop smoking, change your diet, or modify habits that hinder your spiritual growth. Ask, observe, listen. Don't be content with surface knowledge. Go deeper. Let the thought of the incense lead you into your own inner world.

You might meditate on the seven great lights on the altar (in a traditional church there would be six altar candles in addition to an altar cross or crucifix). The flat table surface of the altar represents the pathway you must take through life. The seven lights represents the way stations through which you must pass, assignments that must be met.

The first of these lights represents the Incarnation, that of Jesus, and your own realization as a Christed individual now moving through the earth experiences. The second light might symbolize the Presentation in the temple. It suggests that your faith must move beyond the level of talk. It must be able to stand up as reality in the temple of truth. Is it a productive power? The third light is symbolic of the Transfiguration. Working with that symbol might trigger the development of your own kinetic and telepathic powers. Let your thoughts take you deep within and show you the doors that lead to the chambers of the inner secrets.

The fourth light, the cross, brings to mind the Crucifixion. As Jesus did, so you must also take upon yourself the burdens of those of lower levels of consciousness and help them upward on the ladder of spiritual understanding. Linger in thought until you find the ways and the spiritual means to be an effective teacher. The fifth light is the symbol of the Resurrection. Have you found the secret, the resilience to bounce back from the blows of outrageous fortune, to rise above the karmic limitations of an unpleasant past.

At this point in time that fifth light is not symbolic of your capacity to materialize a physical resurrection, if that is ever to be sought. It has other applications. If you are not able to rise above the physical disorders, dig down into the secret of health. Are you able to rise above every limitation in your path? Are you aware that your current defeats are given to spur you on to greater victories? Why, then, ask, seek, and listen for the secret lore within to teach you the way of conquest. Plan for tomorrow and all your tomorrows. Get the wisdom. Obtain the dynamics to excel your mightiest dreams.

It never fails to amaze me why otherwise intelligent people waste precious time and money on past life readings to determine that in a previous life they were highly placed individuals. If the assumptions claimed on the part of many to have been either a Lincoln, Nefertiti, or a Da Vinci were true it would take a city the size of Los Angeles to provide domicile for all these good but simple fools. Rather than so simply and uselessly, to use time, energy, and meditation, to cut loose the power to help you to greater distinction in this and future lives. Truly, this brand of TM will aid you in this quest.

The fifth light represents the Ascension. Following this lead in continued meditation, it may show you the way to teleportation, levitation, to rise above arrogance and harassments, so much a part of contemporary America. By way of personal note–once in meditation on this theme, I was shown a way for making myself invisible. Show you how? No, find out for yourself.

The seventh light is the symbol of Pentecost. It may show you how to unlock your own power pack, tailor made just for you. It could, if you get down to the real levels of being, show you how to throw away the Jesus crutches, crowning you with your own saviorhood–which is you mighty destiny.

Having found the latch that opens these doors, remain with them in meditation until you have found all the archetypal information they are capable of yielding to you.

For those persons who follow an astrology, the seven great lights follow a still different meditative pattern. The symbolic reality tucked away within these lights could lend you one of the great plenary powers, who are ready to induct their energy resources into your world.

Whether it be the phylacteries of the Jewish faith, the genuflections of Orthodox Christians, or the asanas of Vedanta, all have profound implications for the student of meditation. Those who claim otherwise are simply not well informed.

Chapter 8–Symbols from Far and Near

Religious Symbols, 2006. Used by permission of the artist, Reguly, under Creative Commons Attributions.

The many religions of the world provide an abundance of spiritually significant symbols, each offering a wealth of guidance and inspiration.

In Buddhism, we find the Lord Buddha, the lotus, the thunderbolt, and the wheel. Buddhists, too, have their rosary. Goddard's "Buddhist Bible" offer inspiration, not only for the twenty-eight cycle of the rosary, but for much additional material as well.

As an appetizer, we will give one section of the twenty-eight dealing with the "Supreme Path, The Rosary of Precious Gems."

1. Attach thyself to a religious teacher endowed with spiritual knowledge and power and complete understanding.

2. Seek a delightful solitude endowed with psychic influence, such as a hermitage.

3. Seek friends who have beliefs and habits like your own and in whom thou can place thy trust.

4. Keeping in mind the evils of gluttony, use just enough food to keep fit during the period of retreat.

5. Study the teachings of the great sages of all sects impartially.

6. Study the beneficent sciences of healing and astrology, and the profound art of omens.

7. Adopt such regimen and manner of living as will keep you in good health.

8. Adopt such devotional practices as will be conducive to your spiritual development.

9. Retain such disciples as are firm in faith, meek in spirit, and who appear to be favored by karma in their quest for divine wisdom.

10. Constantly maintain alertness of consciousness in walking, in sitting, in eating, and in sleeping.

These are the ten things to be done.

Christianity offers a plethora of symbols from the cross to pictures of Jesus, the stations of the cross, etc., etc. There is the star of David in Judaism and the crescent and star in Islam. We could mention the methods and symbols suggested by Gurdjieff, the many forms of Kabalistic meditation, and much new material that is surfacing from Sufi sources.

In Hinduism, too, we find seeds to activate the process of meditation. Here we might suggest images of Krishna or Rama, Shiva (Wisdom), Vishnu (Love), Kali (Power), Laksmi (Prosperity), Saraswati (Learning and Skill), and Ganesh (Success).

Attention must always be given to the inner significance of the symbol, which came into being to express the inner nature of truth in some way known only to the meditator.

In conjunction with the use of several of the AUM chants, it might be stimulating to the meditating process to have in a strategic spot, as on a small shrine, the AUM symbol. In fact, the visual aspect of the symbol in its inner use is strengthened if there be a shrine with candles, or just one candle, plus one or more images or symbols.

Perhaps the most popular of eastern symbols, and one of the most effective is the rhythmic repetition of this one:

AUM MANI PADME HUM (Truth is the unity of wisdom and love; may I be united with it).

This mantra can be used in conjunction with other disciplines and modalities or be allowed to be a meditative technique within itself.

The regular practice of audio-visual concentration channels thought along very definite spiritual avenues. It produces a lift in consciousness and brings inspiration to live in tune with the infinite. When a person has sufficiently advanced in the use of specific symbols, they are capable of directing attention to the universal truth underlying all symbols. At that point they are lifted above every stage of idolatry, which still retains some traces in all of us.

Chapter 9–Spiritual Cleansing

Chōzuya (basin for ritual cleansing) at the Meiji Shrine (2006). Used by permission of the photographer, Ray Tsang, under Creative Commons Attribution.

In the extreme extrovert meditation will kindle a kind of introspective self-awareness, which is needed to deepen insight into the deeper values of live. Yet, the extreme introvert will find that meditation not only increases their range of selfless action, it also sharpens their awareness of the reality and significance of the world beyond their immediate reach. Meditation encourages a balanced approach to life. It does aid in the removal of emotional conflicts and psychic tensions.

One of the valued functions of meditation is the work it does in bringing about a psychological house cleaning. When it is properly directed, it will produce a mental catharsis gradually eliminating the unconscious obstructions to the complete functioning of the human personality.

Let us consider a few meditative suggestions that may be used to bring about the balancing and readjustment of our inner mechanisms in accordance with God's superior designs for our lives.

A. A system of self-examination

   1. Preparatory thought of scripture. Search me, O God, and know my heart. Try me. Know me and know my thoughts. See if there be anything wicked in me, and lead me to everlasting life.

   2. A prayer of preparation. Holy, holy, holy, ever living God, infinite in majesty, power and love. I move before you as one filled with awe and humility. Let your grace and strength flow into my life. Let the bright Light of your consciousness scan my real nature and bring my faults to my awareness. Amen.

   3. Self interrogation (pause for reflection after each question). Have I set anything above God as the object of my supreme devotion? Is my life one of continued communion with God? Do I know how to use the Name of God to modify adverse conditions in my world? Am I able to see divinity in all God's people? Am I free to feel with my brother of another faith the strength of his religious devotion?

Do I place into my life periods of spiritual refreshment? Do I devote some time of each day to the cultivation of my spiritual resources?

Is there a desire lurking in my heart to take advantage of anyone? Are my intentions and motives pure and clean? Do I have due revere3nce for the human body as a beautiful temple of God to be kept strong, well, and pure?

Am I honest in all my ethical relationships? Do I use pretenses to gain desirable ends? Do I parade under banners that proclaim something which I inwardly despise? Am I inclined to exaggerate? Do I tend to put the fairest possible construction upon report of evil in others?

Have I subdues the spirit of acquisition and cultivated the spirit of sharing?

Am I willing to surrender to the inner Christ the use of my powers, resources, influence, ambitions, and desires?

4. Complete with the sounding of the following mantra using your own tone, for about fifteen times or longer:

Hagios 'O Theos–Sanctus Deus

Hagios Ischyros–Sanctus Fortis

Hagios Athanatos, eleison hemas.

B. Here, you first read the theme selection very slowly, very thoughtfully. Next, you take a few deep rhythmic breaths. Sound several times, AUM MANI PADME HUM.

Theme: Withdraw into yourself and look. And, if you do not find yourself beautiful as yet, do as the creator of a statue. So, do you also cut away all that is excessive, straighten all that is crooked, bring light to all that is shadowed, labor to make all glow with beauty, and do not cease chiseling your statue until there shall shine out on you the godlike splendor of virtue, until you shall see the final goodness surely established in the stainless shrine (from the Enneads, Plotinus).

After the AUMS, now go over these questions very slowly and meditatively.

I am entering the invisible "I," composed of feelings and thoughts. First, I look at my feelings, emotions. Is each one of them always gracious and pleasant? What feelings did I have when I arose this morning? Was I anxious and irritated? (Analyze this and then proceed).

Are my feelings toward my fellow human beings constructive or otherwise?

Many of our problems are not resolved so much by direct frontal attack, but by the oblique measures that come into play as we reach for more understanding.

This short Hindu prayer is a splendid example for this kind of purpose: "Let us meditate upon the glory of the One who created this universe. Let the Creator illumine our minds."

In these few words we find an immense lake of peace and wisdom to cut us free and allow us to move into moods productive of meditation.

A long and fruitful time of meditation may be had through the thought directing power of this bit of a Shinto prayer: "O Lord, deign to grant me the best that I can live through."

The Gnostic tradition, which has preserved so much of what is truly vital in the Christian faith, a tradition, which now, fortunately is experiencing a revival, offers this meditative theme:

O ruler of Heaven,
O consoler!
Spirit of Truth
Omnipresent and filling everything
Giver of Life!
Come to dwell in us,
Purify us of all iniquity
And save our souls,
O merciful Lord

Chapter 10–Breaking Through to the Light

In the waiting room of the Union Station (1997). Photo in the public domain by virtue of having been taken by a U.S. Government employee taken as part of that person's official duties.

The primary goal, the greatest quest, and the most thrilling aspect in the whole of religion is that brilliant moment of Light and Joy, when we break through into the inner certitude and conviction that we have reached the universal heart of love. It is yours to have and own. You have come forth into this life with a fulltime guarantee that it shall be yours for all time and eternity.

Meditation is the surest road to its realization.

It is not a once and for all type of experience, but something that should recur again and again. It should be a daily thing. There are moments and days when the joy seems far off due to the cyclic currents of life operating in and through you. Yet, still in the heavens.

A short airplane experience up into the sky will always convince you that the sun has not left. Similarly, a time of meditation, of the right sort, can and will fill you into awareness that the Life of Love and Light is still part of your experience.

The capture of the experience may be dependent on many factors. But, as much as anything, it comes by way of a certain kind of meditation I am about to share. The fact that it works for me in rekindling the intensity of the flame, is recharge my spiritual power-pack, to relate me more closely to workable solutions, to replace blind faith with knowing certitude is no reason it will do the same for you. But why don't you try this or something like it for a while and see what happens. Give it a whir.

Start with a basic attitude of surrender and submission. You are planning to focus in on the heart of universal life, certainly a big request. Approach it in the expectant sense of great anticipation you might feel during the count down of your first trip to the moon.

Take your accustomed place of quiet, practice a few deep breaths, read one of the following sentences, and then close your eyes. Let your eyeballs be upturned. Let the meaning of each of these words drop deep into the well of your being.

1. I offer myself to God NOW, wholly and completely.

2. I am not doing anything to find what I am seeking. God is the Doer, the Deed, and the Goal.

3. I invoke the power of God to meditate within me and for me.

4. I surrender my physical existence to the divine will, resolved that my body is no longer a function of my ego but a channel of expression for the divine.

5. I submit my motives, emotions, desires, feelings, and impulses, refusing them the right to pull me hither and yon. They shall be powerful instruments for the release of cosmic love.

6. I surrender my mind to the divine light. I am relentlessly sacrificing and yielding up all dogmatic reasoning, wishful thinking, fixed ideas, and preconceived notions.

7. I wish to be cleansed from all dust of impurity. My self is silently receptive to the self-revelation of the Supreme.

As different thoughts, desires, feelings, and impulses rise up offer them to the divine with the prayer that they may be transmuted into elements of psychic and physical perfection. As deeply buried memories and long forgotten desires emerge into the foreground, observe them, analyze them, offer them to God, as you would your gifts at the altar.

There is no secret in your mind, which cannot be disclosed to the divine. There is no hidden corner of your psyche, which cannot be exposed to the all-seeing eye of God.

Judiciously accept in your life such ideas, contacts, and commitments as are in harmony with cosmic welfare and yours. This would also mean the rejection of ideas and suggestions that are not compatible with your and the cosmic highest good.

You are essentially an active center of the self-expression of Being, not an isolated atom, nor a cell of some social collectivity. You are a unique and creative center of the divine, capable of direct contact with and relation to the Light, Love, and Life of the Cosmos.

A Meditation on Cosmic Love

This modality consists in filling the heart with the spirit of oneness with all existence and in sending out goodwill to the four corners of the map. Contemplation of God as love opens the springs of love in the human heart.

Starting, you send your love to all living creatures, all of them, the snakes and scorpions, the weeds in your garden, the man who left a scar on your soul. Send forth love to all peoples, races, nations of the world, each of which are different manifestations of the one Godhead. Each race, people, nation has a unique contribution to make toward the fulfillment of God's cosmic pattern and program.

Finally, send forth your love to all human beings, friend, foe, kindred, alien, and the indifferent ones. Imagine yourself as a sort of Sputnik in carrying love, affection, helpfulness, and joy to each of these people. Divine love is not coercive but persuasive. It is not aggressive or tyrannical but persuasive. It is not possessive or domineering but patiently concerned in the beloved's free growth and welfare. It is not intolerant of other's failing and shortcomings but understanding of the travail of soul making. While thinking of foes or foreigners, do remember they also dwell with you in the same Cosmic Self.

Hatred and hostility are not answers to any situation. They only deepen the problem. Hatred only confirms enmity. It exudes poison. It recoils as a boomerang. Only love has the power to break the

54

vicious circle of hate, hostility, and resentment. It disarms opposition, thaws cold relations, turns apathy into response, and converts enmity into friendship.

It is most important that this meditation be applied to life. It must be lived. Apply it at home, in the street, while at the office, practicing the Presence of God in all you see.

This modality is based on a vision of the spiritual unity of all existence. According to the fundamental spiritual intuition of humankind, all specific forms of existence are significant modes of manifestation of the same creative energy of Being.

Chapter 11–Comparative Views of Meditation

"Kyoto Meditation Room." Copyright © 2006, Joi Ito. Used and adapted by permission of the photographer under Creative Commons Attribution.

The functions and objectives of meditation may be illustrated diagrammatically to good effect. This type of presentation also points up the relative values and benefits of different forms of meditation may be expected to yield.

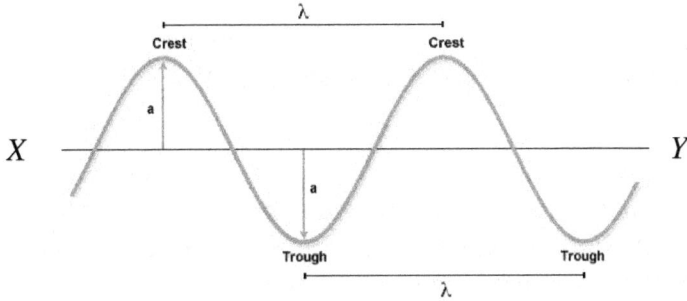

In this diagrammatical scheme the straight line, X-Y, represents the median line of average, normal, balanced responsiveness to life. The peaks (called "crests" in wave terminology) indicate the high points in life–exultation–somewhat indicative of aspects of the manic phase of life, a type of positive elation.

The low points in the diagram are the valleys (called "troughs" in wave terminology). These indicate depression, or dejection–experiences that crop up when life is lived less optimally.

It would be assumed, and rightly so, that living a steady life on the X-Y axis is to be preferred to life on a roller coaster between peaks and valleys. Who wants these downward swings into unhappiness, these dark nights of the soul! True, the roller coaster effect does give us moments of unexcelled bliss. But, then, these alleys are always a kind of descent into hell.

Most gurus are quite agreed that the way to live is to try for that median line. Give up the peaks in order to escape the valleys. It is the classical view of the value of meditation. To use Hindu terms, we sacrifice the *anandas* (blissful experiences), the *shantis* (the peaceful ones), and the *samadhis* (spiritual state of consciousness), in order that we might escape the tamas (darkness) and dukha (suffering).

Transcendental Meditation, TM, operates somewhat differently. While it still presents a fluctuating curve, the low troughs of the valleys are leveled off. It offers richer fruits as a reward, or end, of the labors inherent in meditation.

Again referring the diagram, above, TM moves toward the development of a new X-Y axis near the peaks, or crests, of the wave. It also strives for much smaller downward fluctuations. As one continues in meditation, moving toward the transcendental field, the axis will rise higher and higher as the valleys become less and less pronounced.

From this point of view alone it would seem that TM represents an advance over more classical forms of meditation. My own findings suggest that the peaks, under normal conditions, should not be considered as rosy Pollyannaisms. In TM, we presume the presence of a divine process that is always at work. Even as one seeks to approach God in meditation, so, in like manner the divine also seeks and finds the individual. And, Divine intelligence operates within the individual. In TM, one is always at work selecting only those mental states, which are conducive to constructive living. As one moves between the circumference of life, where a person typically functions, and the center of Being, where individual divinity exists, there is constant feedback, which helps the practitioner move toward maximum mental growth and stability.

These findings are based on my work and association with so-called average, or "normal," people. I doubt my findings would be equally applicable to troubled, hysterical, or highly neurotic individuals. Persons so afflicted should probably restrict their practice to more conventional forms of meditation, unless they have a competent and trained guide.

While these observations about the relative values of TM apply to most of its many forms, the positive benefits I have stated are enhanced when symbols are used in the process of meditation. In speaking of symbols, I am referring particularly to those rooted in the experience of our species. Since they reach into the archetypal strata of individual consciousness they tend to relate to individual consciousness, and have the advantages of being able to offer the kind of support that is produced by abiding values.

If you are aware of astrological symbols, each one of them would be a valuable aid. The AUM symbol, shown below, either by itself or as surrounded by a cluster of astrological symbols, would be a valid tool. For greater effectiveness, you might like to reproduce the one that appears below on a larger scale.

The Aum, a symbol of Hinduism. This image consists entirely of information that is common property and is therefor in the public domain.

Other religious symbols are reproduced below. Reflect on each. Perhaps one or more them have a special appeal to you.

The Buddhist wheel of karma. This image consists entirely of information that is common property and is therefor in the public domain.

The hand, symbol of the Jain faith tradition. Image released into the public domain by the artist, Amakuha.

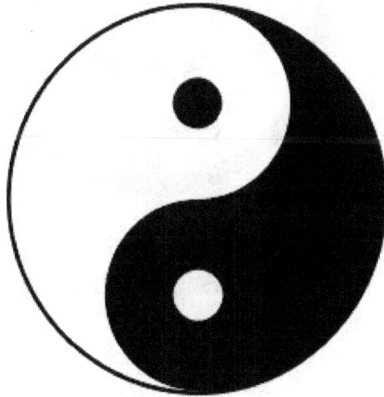

The conjoined yin and yang of Taoist philosophy. This image consists entirely of information that is common property and is therefor in the public domain.

Temple gate, symbol of the native Japanese Shinto religion. Used by permission of the author, MesserWoland, under Creative Commons Attribution.

Jewish menorah. Released by the artist, Frater5, into the public domain.

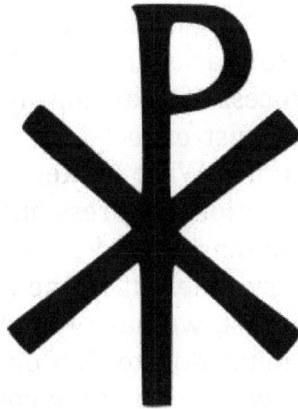

The Christian Chi Rho, first two letters of Christ's name. This image is the Unicode character 2627, and is in the public domain.

The star and crescent of Islam. This image consists entirely of information that is common property and is therefor in the public domain.

The use of proper symbolism in meditation moves the individual on an ascending line, the ascent broken from time to time by short valleys and small downward dips. These occasional rest stops and tiny set backs are no more than part of the ordinary process of cleansing and readjustment that each of us must expect in the course of our journey through life. What matters is not so much that there are occational depressions but that there is opportunity for marked and steady advancement. It is the efficiency inherent in the ascent patterns that matters. At last, we have found the means to make the real injunction to, "go on from more to more." It is a way which is fully cooperative with the evolutionary scheme. Yes, and it is the fulfillment of holy dreams–to make our lives an endless chain of prayer and the key to celestial living.

Chapter 12–And What About Me?

Archives of the Mennonite Board of Missions. In the public domain.

Our materialistic age has dulled our appetite and stifled our zeal for real and nourishing spiritual food. Humankind seems to have lost its taste for the kind nutritional food that would help us evolve according to the pattern destined for us. "What's in it for me?" is the bestial cry of a dehumanized people. "Give me some quick results" "Let the way be easy" "May the taste be pleasant" "Make sure the rewards are immediate and great." The sentiments expressed here is all that seems to matter to folks these days. These basic attitudes run through all levels of society, however well disguised. It is an ethos that is deeply entrenched even in the spiritual institutions of our day.

You cannot escape these views when taking a look at the so-called "New Thought" churches. Both lecture platform and printed page ooze with the noxious exudates of this crass and cancerous preoccupation with hedonistic materialism.

But hold on, there is a whole range of "churches" not exempt from this charge, although their approach is cloaked in the language of cheap theology. What they call "personal salvation" is their principal stock in a shop-worn trade. They give leave to anyone to live like hell, but offer heaven in exchange for a deathbed conversion. Really, they are compounding a mix of evil "karma"–dragon's teeth that will return for a frightful harvest.

No, "personal salvation" is not my thing. I *am* interested in showing the way to personal illumination; using methods of purification; gaining knowledge about never-ending growth in mind, heart, soul, and spirit; finding ways to handle social problems that lead to real solutions; achieving consciousness about an everlasting life that can begin right now; and finding companionship as we move along on the currents of life. If along the way (and you may very will experience this) you get help handling your problems, be happy. But, don't look for this as a result of meditation. Put the "kingdom" first. Let the rest of it "just" happen. And it will, if you let it.

Earlier, we suggested that some personal gains would accrue as a result of meditation. And that is true. We did so in order to help you know that there are ways of one's present dilemmas. Now, we add that solutions to these temporal vexations must never be more than by-products of spiritual practice.

In my estimation, to make personal salvation your end goal and aim in life is a self-defeating striving for an odd type of material satisfaction. It is not the highest and best good for a person to seek out. Listen instead to the words of Matthew 5:48, "Be perfect, therefor, as your heavenly Father is perfect."

66

Chapter 13–The Ultimate Theological Deception

Wall art seen in Vancouver, BC, Canada (2009). Released into the public domain by the photographer.

Chapter 13 is another brief one. Like the previous chapter, it is short enough to have fitted in somewhere else. However, the message of both chapters is so crucial to the whole topic of meditation that we didn't want it to get lost interspersed among other ideas.

The ultimate theological deception, sometimes called the Great Lie of the West, is this: Life, liberation, salvation, the blessed assurance, the Peace that passes all understanding, the breakthrough into the Light, is dependent on some kind of belief, some dogmatic assertion, or a theological formula.

This contention and belief is a hundred and eighty degrees from the truth. The matter of belief holds an insignificant and miniscule relationship to whatever magnitude of spiritual certitude to which you may aspire. The less your mind is cluttered with dogmas, beliefs, "theologisms," the greater is your hope for the for the attainment of inner Knowledge and the Light of divine Truth.

Jesus said, "He that doeth ... shall know." A verbal and creedal faith is a dead faith, unless the verbalization arises from the inner Light of personal discovery. The Way, the technique, the methods known by true teachers and gurus preceded, by a long way, dogmatic beliefs and teachings. In meditation, we teach many aspects of the Way, any one of which is sufficient to get one through.

Approach your meditation pilgrimage with a wide, wide, open mind, willing, if need be, to yield up and surrender the faith you have held. In its place, a new and far more vital discovery will come. It will be *your* way and philosophy, and not that of another.

Listen to Swami Prabavananda, a great teacher of the twentieth century:

Have nothing to do with any theory, dogma, or presupposition. Even whether you believe in God does not matter. Belief in God is not a necessary prerequisite for the spiritual life. Religion is experience. Whatever you have of theories or of preconceived ideas or, even if you believe in God, is not important to the seeker after Truth who follows certain principles and makes the experiment. The Truth will be revealed because Truth is Truth, an existent factor, not anything imaginary, but a matter of experience.

What God is, what Reality is, nobody has been able to express in words. To define God is to limit Him, to finitize Him. Belief in God is a means but not the only means by which to reach ultimate Reality.

The way to learn to swim is not by reading a book and debating it. Get into the water and try it.

Chapter 14—Invisible Helpers

In the New Testament letter to the Hebrews, we find an oft-quoted assurance, "We are surrounded by a cloud of witness."

The fact of this truth has been born in on me with force sufficient to call it a fact. We are surrounded by witnesses, and never by more competent help than when we are in meditation. No, I do not stand alone in this assertion. Many of the most competent observers in the field of psychic research have met this phenomenon and talked about it at length.

Those who seek the center of truth, the glory of the inner Light, who would seriously replace beliefs with solid certitudes will find in association with them, on inner planes, at least one devoted ally. The reason that this ally has become a part of your life will, in time, set you apart from and make you more effective than other people.

This ally will join you. For a time, you will work without knowledge of your ally's presence. In time, you will become conscious of this being. Yes, you will even form a friendship with it. You will learn to trust this being and the direction provided. If you are fortunate, you may, eventually, even see him with an inner eye. But, its phenomenological is not really even important.

This ally has the capacity to take you and transport you in consciousness beyond the limitations and boundaries of yourself and thus allow you to transcend, or ascend, the realm of ordinary reality.

As you continue your journey as a devoted and serious pilgrim on the spiritual path, you will find that this ally has no physical form and cannot be ascertained with physical means. It would be best for you to think of your ally as a quality, presence, or attribute that has been given to you and added to your life, and not so much as a person.

This ally, when it first appears is your orbit, existing shy as a deer by the side of the road. But as you continue faithfully in your spiritual work and follow through on the hints it sends your way, it will become increasingly attached to you. We might say, that this ally is an aspect of Deity, set aside, ordained, sanctified, and sent forth to further your spiritual evolution. It may be possible that it can be perceived in ways other than that of meditation. However, the only other evidence I have found for its presence has been during times when I have been engaged in sacramental activity.

In addition to it (1) being formless, the ally is (2) a quality, that will establish for you're a series of (3) rules. And this aspect is difficult to describe. You will find certain instructions coming to you, some of which have the feel of having a procedural aspect. Others are more personal in nature. They may have to do with your actions, behavior, regulation, and attitude. Since they are never identical for any two people, each person having a different ally, any description given here would be misleading. (4), it will be closer to you than anyone you know—even to the point of enlarging your capacities for precognition.

Chapter 15—Last Minute Tips

We've now told our story and had our say. Thinking of our visit together, I find myself jumping at questions, questions, and more questions that may or may not be on your mind. Any questions you have are good and intelligent questions, too. Should I attempt to answer them? Of course I will.

When to and when not to meditate? What to do and what not to do?

Wait for an hour or two after meals. Never meditate if you have been exposed to a considerable amount of tobacco smoke. If you are a smoker, wait at least two hours after your last smoke before attempting to meditate. If you have consumed alcohol, or other mind-altering substances, wait at least two hours before attempting to meditate. In short, wait until it is out of your system.

If you have a serious cold, fever, or acute pain, let these pass before you begin.

With respect to positions, for our purposes it would be best to use a simple, straight-backed, chair. Sit in an erect position.

Avoid intensive reading just before or during meditation.

Take a few deep breaths in a rhythmic fashion. Much is to be said for a variety of breathing exercises. But, this is not the place and time.

Your exercises should be performed as often as you can afford the time. Once a day should be the minimum. If you let too many days go by, the cumulative effects will dissipate. Let three days elapse without meditation and you will be clearly out of practice.

What if you cannot arrange a suitable setting, such as room, time, etc.? Meditation is simply not for you.

When you are having difficulty quieting and training your mind, you might try this prayer, "O Lord, take away this mortal, imperfect, mind, and be gracious enough to give me even the smallest ray of Your Light."

It is nearly useless to meditate when you are tired. Your body must be a balanced, healthy, and rested condition for this kind of work.

Don't talk about the spiritual discipline you have embarked upon, at least not at first, unless those with whom you discuss it are understanding and sympathetic.

I have seen as many non-vegetarian meditators as I have seen vegetarians. It seems to make little difference as far as the effectiveness is concerned. Do, however, follow a good and sensible diet.

What about sexual relations? So, what about it? Should it have any limiting effect on meditation? No. Actually, it seems to help. I have not been able to determine that celibacy has any particular advantages with respect to meditation. Perhaps, we should realize that sex is here to stay. It is a normal part of being a creature of God, and can be an ally. In my estimation, most of what has been written on this subject, pro and con, is mostly nonsense anyhow.

The best time for your exercises is morning and evening. But you will have to work that out for yourself. If you are interested in magical practices, do not divert meditation for that purpose. There are many occult ways that are much more certain and safer.

AUF WIEDERSEHEN

And so, we bid you farewell. Your visit is appreciated. Keep in touch, please. Let us help and serve you. And remember, meditation consists of gradually wiping the dust from the mental or psychic mirror through a process of concentration on spiritual truth, and the regulation of life's affair in accordance with spiritual ideals.

The sun of spiritual illumination shines out when the clouds of ignorance and the mists of desire are cleared away from the firmament of consciousness.

Meditation is a gradual process of transition, by means of disciplined effort, from bondage to freedom, from ignorance to knowledge, from mediate mental cognition to immediate spiritual realization.

ABOUT ASCENSION

The Ascension Alliance and Community of Ascensionists is a religious organization and clerical congregation; part of a spiritual movement and of the one Mystical Body of Christ; a Church; an umbrella organization; and an expression of God's mystical movement of Spirit. We draw our lineage, or lines of apostolic succession, from the historic churches, East and West, although we are not a part of the Roman Catholic or Eastern Orthodox communions. We derive our chief western line through the Old Catholic churches of Europe, which separated from the see at Rome beginning in the early 1700s. Our principal eastern line comes through the ancient churches of India, which are believed to have been established by the Apostle Thomas, beginning in the year 52, C.E., and which were served by Assyrian and Syrian Orthodox bishops for generations. We like to think of ourselves as being born of a "free" Catholic (or universal) vision and a much larger stirring of Spirit, which beckons us to transcend old ways that no longer work, ascend to higher levels of consciousness, and be transformed. In addition, we are dedicated to helping other seekers who wish to do the same.

We Joyfully Celebrate the Sacraments in Communities Worldwide

Mailing Address:
P.O. Box 167, Vaughn, WA 98394

Website: ascensionalliance.org